HOW TO WRITE A SHORT STORY

Beginner's Easy Way to Create and Write a Story from Scratch

Abraham Adekunle

How to Write a Short Story

Copyright © 2016 by Abraham Adekunle.

Book and Cover design by Abe A.

ISBN-13: 978-1533336293
ISBN-10: 1533336296

Second Edition: May 2016

10 9 8 7 6 5 4 3 2

CONTENTS

The Ultimate Guide on How to Write a Short Story

INTRODUCTION

WE ARE NOW in a technological age, where even teenagers decide what they do. One of those things is writing. People write for different reasons. Some write...

- ...to kill boredom and accompany themselves.
- ...to live another life.
- ...for the joy of it, and so on.

Whatever your choice is to write, writing will take you places, mentally, success-related, and maybe even financially. But you've chosen to read this book simply because you want to write fiction, and write to perfect the art. One little tip to achieve that is to write more often and ship it to the world—your readers, your publisher, your blog, wherever. You'll notice that you're getting better with each one. Now to fiction.

Fiction writing is a type of writing that makes unreal events real. It is not real, but your readers want it to appear real to them. That is what this book will teach you.

From characters to settings, to plots, to dialogues, you're all good to go. Or, you don't even know what those things are? Don't worry. It's explained in detailed. Sometimes, explanation may not be the key to understanding. That is why, in addition to my succinct explanation, I have given clear examples, of which some are visual. I even included some excerpts from my personal stories, so that you can understand better.

As you follow this book at heart, I wish you success with your first, or whatever number, story. Cheers.

CHAPTER *1*

ESSENTIALS OF FICTION

INTRODUCTION

The Ultimate Guide on How to Write a Short Story

LIKE HUMANS NEED oxygen, there are some vital elements a story (which is here, referred to as fiction) needs. It is simply: character, conflict, and setting. In a story, something has to happen to someone, somewhere, sometimes.

For easy understanding, these essentials of fiction are like the blades of a ceiling fan. They are equidistant from each other. You start with one; you're bound to meet the other two, if you want your work to be a story. Again, you can start with an idea of one; definitely, you'll get the other two in no time.

How Stories Are Conceived

As said earlier, stories are born out of a writer's imagination choices. The production of a story begins with any of the three elements mentioned.

For example, a writer may start with a character idea. A lost boy in an uninhabited jungle. Then, the ideas for conflict and settings starts setting in. What made the boy lost? Where was the jungle located? Was there a telephone at that time? What time of the day did he get lost? Would he be found before the dark? Or would he use another day lurking around there, hungry and naked?

Now, answers are different. It depends on the writer. A writer may situate the jungle in Austin, Texas, New York. Another may situate it in Australia. While another may situate it in Congo.

For example, a writer's choice might go like this: A lost boy in an uninhabited jungle in Austin. He wandered off unknowingly from the highway when the car he and his mother were traveling in broke down. The mother has gone to find help somewhere and had left the boy there. (If you're a smart writer with great imagination, you should have noticed another story idea popping out from that scene. A careless mother. If the story would be in part, that other idea might make another part.)

Another writer may start with setting

ideas.

What Settings Are

Settings are the place and time a story takes place. For example, one of my stories, Beyond Her Boundary, took place in Ohafia Village, Abia State, Nigeria, spanning a duration of a day. The other day involved was just a headline news.

As a writer, you can start with these ideas too.

For example, your setting may be in a Friday the 13th cabin in the night. Who are/is inside the cabin? Why are they there?

A common answer may be: Julie and Hattie were inside the Friday the 13th cabin, scared. It was a night. They were hungry, but they couldn't cook inside the small cabin, or they'll die of suffocation.

From that answer, we can deduce the characters as Julie and Hattie. The time of the day was the night. The place was inside a cabin. Maybe it was even the rain outside that caused them to shiver. The conflict they were battling was hunger and inability to cook in the small cabin. Maybe fear of the dark was even included.

Yet, another writer can start with a conflicting idea.

The conflict may be a man trembling while driving home because he was going to kill his wife or send her to jail. Other questions may then come in. Like, who was the husband? Who was the wife? Where was the home mentioned earlier? What did the wife do to deserve that furious decision? Where do they live? Where was the man driving home from?

Self-assessment 1

Begin with a character, conflict or setting idea. After conceiving, ask burning questions that will reveal the other two elements. You can use the questionnaire at the chosen element below.

CHARACTER

There are people in a story or something that are personified. These are the people that interact. These are the people that something happens to. These are the people your readers care about. They want to know what happens to them next. Sometimes, it may be personified animals, like the ones in George Orwell's Animal Farm. In other words, they put themselves in the character's shoe. As a result, be really careful with the way you develop your characters. It may be the reason a reader will stop reading your short story, forever.

Before we move on, let's examine these types of characters.

Hero/Heroine/Protagonist... is also referred to as the main, major or central character of a story. The storyline depends on he or she. When she interacts with other characters in the story, we understand the story better. He or she, like in movies, is the good character readers don't want anything to happen to. This is the character that wants to go about his or her business in peace. But everything cannot be rosy. In fact, it mustn't be rosy, especially in a story. That's why there has to be...

Antihero/Anti-heroine/Antagonist... is the character that is mainly opposing the protagonist in a story. Their course opposes. What they believe contradict each other. In some great thriller stories, the antagonist consciously pursues the protagonist in any way. This character's main purpose is to undermine the works of the protagonist. Almost all the time, an antagonist bear evil qualities and their vision is also evil.

...a character that has his or her name used to name the title of the story is an **Eponymous Character**. The philosophy is simple: the name of either the protagonist or antagonist is the title of the short story. Most times, the name is also included in a phrase to give it more meaning.

...a character who is unreceptive to

changes is a Flat **Character**. This character only maintains a static personality throughout the story and it is easy for readers to know what he or she will do next.

Round Character: This character, as the name suggests, is given all-round information in the story. You can write a short biography of this kind of characters because their description is very detailed and in-depth. This is usually attributed to the main character of a story. A main character has more stage time than anyone else in the story. Unlike flat characters, round characters are difficult to predict.

How to Characterize

Characterization simply means introducing a character and his or her personality in a story. In order to create a character, a writer must have an in-depth knowledge of him or her. (To create an in-depth profile of your characters, use the character questionnaire.) As a writer, you have the full control of your character in your hands. It depends on you the way you introduce them, make them make a mistake, or even kill them. There are three ways to introduce a character in a story: naming, showing, telling.

Naming: This method involves naming a character to invoke a sense of imagination. In one of my stories, I wrote:

> Behind the computer desks, a huge monitor hung on a wall a few inches from the floor, where different areas of the barracks were being monitored. The operator in the middle was the control room boss. His name was Ikechuckwu. He'd had his spirit pulled down by the General, but he wouldn't let that get to him.

With that, we know that the man was a boss with people under him and we sense the technological kind of work he does. And we know his name, too.

Showing: this technique involves the use

of actions of the characters. Even without naming some of my characters in one of my stories, readers could still be able to sense that, "Oh, the policeman is a wicked and professional liar."

Telling: This involves plain telling of a character's information. This usually is a succinct summary of it.

How to Generate Character Ideas

Observation: If you are born with a writer trait, you would've noticed that characters observe a lot. From their neighbors to the street hawkers, to the sellers and buyers in the marketplace. You also need to observe if you want ideas to seamlessly flow to you. Ask the following questions as you observe:

- What kind of person does this person feel to me? Why?

- How does different age groups dress in the marketplace? What about the school? Church?
- What kind of things do they buy? That makes them a what? Vegetarian? Smoker? A heavy sugar and cholesterol consumer, despite obese status?
- What gadgets do they use? A telephone? A TV set? A desktop or Laptop computer? Or a freaking old, worn-out radio that creaks with every millisecond of sound?
- How do they behave? Irritated? Angry all the time? Fearless?
- What do they talk about? Politics? Sports? Latest fashion? Hacking and technology?

Imagination: God gave us six senses. The sixth sense is our imagination. With it, we can daydream about our to-be-character.

What do you imagine when you hear or say the name, "Hattie?" I imagine a twenty-something-year-old blond woman, who wears button-down and skirts all the time and works part-time in a restaurant.

What about the name, "Bryne?" For me, I imagine a 25-year-old brunette guy who flies a helicopter.

Your Hattie is different and so is your Bryne. Your Hattie may be a sixty-four-year-old widow who teaches kids at school, doesn't think of retiring, and has a quick stride as if she'd visit the restroom the next minute. Your Bryne may be a man with four kids and a wife who's about to divorce him, and who's also in a risk of losing his lucrative job because of his integrity against compromise.

Newspapers and Magazine: there are true stories written in dailies every day. If you can spare some bucks to buy one or have an old issue at home, grab it and extract the characters in the event. Let's say a story was written about a woman who killed her maid because according to her, "I caught her having sex with my husband."

Now, your work is to change the names of

the woman, her maid, and her husband. You can even extract only the conflict there, the maid having an affair with her husband. Then, use the character questionnaire to create a profile each for the husband, the woman, and the maid.

Movies: Movies has lots and lots of character ideas you can use in your story. You may not want to use their full personality but just a tiny bit of them.

When you watch a movie, think about the physique of a character, attitude and behavior, routine, families, and relationships, properties owned, etc.

Create more from less: There is a huge tree in a mustard seed that even a bird can perch on. That means, from one of your characters, you can create other characters.

For example, if your character is a gentle and meek woman who loves peaceful things and atmosphere. Her husband may just be a freaking wife beater. Their conflict may even be that the woman loves him and couldn't bear leaving him, yet he beats her every day.

Another example may be a rich lady who works in Victoria Island, Lagos. Because people give more prestige to people working in that area, men run after her every day, perhaps most of them are poor. You can create another set of characters, let's say, two men, one rich and the other poor. The poor has difficulty seeing her for even a second; while the rich can just invite her to anywhere and throw a mouth-blowing party for her.

Other ways to generate character ideas are from **books, pictures, etc.**

How to Create a Character

Without questions, fiction would lack originality. Characters in a story are to be created. That is why writing is a craft that enables you to create something with the tools you have. Without much ado, if you want to create a character, you can either let your imagination run wild and pen down confusing information or use a character questionnaire and get straight to the point.

(**Note:** there is no wrong or right way to use the below character questionnaire. You decide and it shall be so.)

- What's your character's name? (**Character idea:** Like I said before, you can get an idea for your character profiles with imagination. Let's say that your Bryne is 25 years old and flies a helicopter. You can then complete the character questionnaire if you need more information or generate conflict and setting ideas. Conflict idea: Bryne is asked to carry out a transport mission for the army. Setting idea: army cantonment where Bryne would take off the helicopter with soldiers; and a forest where a war would happen.)
- What's your character's age?
- Occupation? (**Character idea:** Your character is passionate about an op-

posite gender's occupation. **Conflict**: No one wants to employ him or her, and your character is keen on getting that kind of job, no matter the workaround.)

- Sex?
- Where does your character live? (**Character idea**: Your character is fearful because he or she lives in a haunted house, inherited from parents. **Conflict**: Your character does not have anywhere to live except that house because she's in debt and so she has to face the horror. **Setting**: A haunted house.)
- Who does your character live with?
- Is your character tall or dwarf?
- What's his or her hair color?
- Eye color?
- Does your character have a beard? What kind? (**Character idea**: Your female character grows a beard. **Conflict**: She shaves it clean every day without any hint of her growing beard exposed to anybody. Howev-

er, she goes on holiday somewhere far from home without remembering to bring along her required toiletries for proper shaving.)

- Does your character have muscle?
- What kind of dress does your character have in his or her wardrobe? What kind does he or she wear on specific days? (**Character idea**: Your character has a flair for fashion and latest clothes. **Conflict**: Tour character's train for a date is due in a few minutes and the clothes she has just ordered hasn't arrived. **Character idea**: Your character wears jeans for tedious tasks to cope with the "wear and tear" of the fabrics he used and for the "wear and tear" of his flesh. **Conflict**: One day, he lost his way on a highway in the night. He decides to go a little farther into the bush to pass the night, but tedious, horrific tasks are awaiting him. But he's got no jean anywhere in sight right now.)

- What are your character's strengths? Weaknesses?
- Talents?
- Does your character plan ahead? Or your character lives his life spontaneously the way it comes?
- Is your character neat or dirty? Organized or not?
- What would make your character compromise his or her qualities?
- What are your character's beliefs? Superstitions?
- How does your character talk? Fast? Slowly?
- How would you describe his speech? Choppy? Flowing? Is he or she a stutterer?
- How is his or her vocabulary? Does he or she blow enormous grammar? Or does he or she use simple words?

- Is your character in a relationship? (Married, engaged, divorced, or dating?)

- Who are your character's family? (Father, mother, siblings, aunts, uncles?)
- Who are your character's friends? Best friends?

- What does your character possess? (Cars, houses, bank accounts, pets, books, etc.)
- What is in your character's desk drawer? Bookshelf?
- What are in your character's refrigerator? What about kitchen cupboard?
- What property or properties does your character value most? (**Character idea:** Your character values his laptop computer dearly. **Conflict:** Your character's house got burnt while he was out.)

- Can your character control his or her temper?
- In what case will your character kill? For a family member? For a spouse?

- Where does your character feel irritated? What makes he or she feel irritated?
- Does your character entertain guests in his or her house? Or does your character like his or her privacy?
- Is your character shy? Or outgoing?
- Is your character approachable?
- Is your character confident? Fearless?
- Is your character polite or rude?
- What makes your character feel lazy or stay indoor all day?
- Does your character asks for what he or she needs straightaway or wait for a trigger?
- In what situation does your character feel erotic?
- Does your character smoke or not?
- Does your character take alcohol?

- Who was your character's first love?
- Who did your character grow up with?

- What brings your character's memories back? What are the memories?
- What are your character's favorites? Color? Sporting club? Books? Drinks? TV program?

Note: Please note that this questionnaire is meant to trigger your imagination. If you feel there are areas that it didn't cover, feel free to add yours. You can even create your own custom character questionnaire and use it anyhow you like. That's creative writing for you. You are always in charge of the creation.

Self-assessment 2

If you have conceived a character idea in self-assessment 1, now is the time to create a full profile of your character using the above questionnaire.

If you have also conceived either of conflict or setting ideas, use the character questionnaire to create a profile for the characters that will evolve from it.

CONFLICT

Conflict is what causes a problem in a story. It is what makes the story thrilling, fun and enjoyable. Conflict ideas are easy to conceive but subtle to include in a story. For example, if you use a conflict idea that has been around for a decade, readers will start showing you the way out of their time. Say you want to write a romance story and you follow the good ol'

Boy falls in love with a girl.

Girl accepts boy.

An antagonist who's hellbent on sabotaging the boy kidnaps the girl.

Then the boy saves the girl.

And they live happily ever after.

Oh, have you been dozing at hearing it already? Storylines that tends to evolve around those kinds of ideas are blunt. You need to think smart and wise.

There   is   no   one   straight-shot

questionnaire that works for getting conflict ideas. You just have to look at your character and setting from your own perspective. Ask questions like:

- What does your character want badly that he or she can't get? Or that his her weakness is getting in the way? For example, your character may be passionate about an opposite gender's occupation, but his or her gender is sabotaging her ability to get a job related to the occupation.
- What does your character struggle with? For example, stage freight.
- Who wants to kill your character or sabotage his or her business? For example, a partner in business that wants to inherit all the business' asset.

Note: Please note that this questionnaire is meant to trigger your imagination. If you feel there are areas that it didn't cover, feel free to add yours. You can even create your own custom conflict questionnaire and use it anyhow you like. That's creative writing for you. You are always in charge of the creation.

Self-assessment 3

Ask questions that reveal conflict ideas and answer them.

SETTING

Setting is the physical and social environment within which characters function. Setting descriptions are weaved into stories so that it flows well. In this kind of situation, figures of speech work best, as it helps you, the writer, to present a clear pictorial presentation in your story.

When talking about setting, three things are referred to:

- **The physical setting:** This comprises of the neighborhood, town, village, city, etc., which the story took place in. For example, a physical setting of a story may be an army cantonment, an over-occupied house, or a cattle ranch.

- **The social environment**: This includes the language, culture, and the social condition of the physical setting. It deals with the way they interact and associate with each other.

- **The period of time:** what I mean by the period of time is the duration the story lasted and the time of the day each scene took place. For example, the period of time of a story could be in the night, spanning a duration of all night and ending in the morning. In one of my stories, the duration lasted for just a day.

How to Generate Historical Setting

Ideas

Historical stories are stories that are set in the history. Just like other elements of a story, a historical setting idea also needs to be generated. Anything your character does, touch, see, smell, and hear depends on your setting. Below are ways you can generate historical setting ideas:

- **Interviews:** If you want to set your story in a setting that's historical, interviews are a great way to go. You can do some interview yourself and find some online.

- **Books:** Not only that books written in a certain period are for people in that period of time, it also captures a great deal of the setting information at that time. I wanted to carry on a project of writing a story set in 1980 Nigeria. I had to find some local books to get the kind of atmosphere it was then.

- **Journals:** Journals aren't just public rants; they're specific case studies and documentations of things pertaining to a subject matter. How great would it be to find a dedicated journal, both online and offline, that underscores subjects that happen in your setting? That's a goldmine of setting ideas.

- **Movies:** Movies help you both in your visual sense and in your hearing sense. Movies set in the period you want your story to happen helps a lot. You can see how the setting looks like and what kind of sound it issues.

How to Create a Setting Profile for Your Story

When you imagine a setting in your brain, chances are some tiny bit of information you need escapes you. But with questions, you'll just have to imagine the right thing the first time.

Physical Setting

Basically, what you need to ask in this section is:

Where did the story take place?

How does it look like, smell like, feels like? What kind of sound is being emitted there?

Below are the main questions put in place to help you with your imagination.

- What's the name of the neighborhood, town, city, village that the story took place? In what state and country?
- What kinds of houses are there in the neighborhood?
- What kind of house does your character live in?
- What does your character's bedroom look like? Living room? Bathroom? Attic?

- What are in your character's wardrobe? Desk drawer? Safe? Attic?
- What does your character's study look like?
- What does your character's yard look like? What are in the yard?
- What does your character's workplace look like? Where is it located?
- Does your character have his or her office? If yes, is it organized or scattered? (**Note:** In the character questionnaire, there's a question whether your character is organized or not. It has to match this. If he or she is organized, then the office looks neat and tidy. If not, it looks scattered, littered and shabby. **Conflict idea:** If your character is organized and neat and she met her office scattered and dirty, she could be suspicious. Someone might have searched her office. Who? When? You decide.)

Social Environment

- What language do they speak in the neighborhood, town, city or village? (**Conflict idea**: Suppose your character lives in a neighborhood where people don't speak English and she does. Maybe she would walk up to someone and say something in English that the person would misinterpret and stir up a fight.)
- What kind of culture is it there?
- Where do people involuntarily meet to interact? E.g. schools, church, etc.
- Where do they voluntarily go to interact? E.g. clubhouse, stadium, museum, theater, cinema, market, shopping mall?
- What are the culture's marriage prerequisites? Dating prerequisite?
- At what age are teenagers legally free, according to the culture?
- What kind of festivals do they celebrate?

- How do they dress up?

Duration

- What is the length of the story? E.g. a day, two months, etc.
- When did each scene take place?

Note: Please note that these questionnaires are meant to trigger your imagination. If you feel there are areas that it didn't cover, feel free to add yours. You can even create your own custom setting questionnaire and use it anyhow you like. That's creative writing for you. You are always in charge of the creation.

Self-assessment 4

From your character or conflict ideas, create a setting that suits it from the above questionnaire.

SUMMARY

In this chapter you have learned:

- ...how stories are conceived.
- ...the three essential elements of a story and how to generate their ideas.

Self-assessment 5

At this point, you should have at least complete character profile(s), conflict ideas, and a setting that suits it. If you don't have it yet now, go back to the previous self-assessment tests and complete them.

CHAPTER *2*

PLOTTING 101

INTRODUCTION

In mathematics, graphs are plotted. They follow patterns. For example, the quadratic graph is either a U-shaped or n-shaped graph.

Linear graphs are always straight. Sine and cosine graphs slope upward and downward like a snake. For those graphs, those are their patterns, they can't change.

The main reason plot is introduced to story writing is that you can start the presentation wherever you like. For example, I may decide to plot the tip of the "U" or "n" first before any other point. And I may start from the either side.

In stories, it's similar. You can start a story from wherever you wish, even from the end. The conflict is just to get the story out in whole like a graph would be no matter where you start plotting it.

Plotting then refers to the act of giving a story a structure. **Plot,** however, refers to the structure of a story.

We can plot stories in only two ways: chronological and episodic.

CHRONOLOGICAL PLOTTING

Chronological Plotting, also called **organic or linear plotting,** is the act of structuring a story from start to finish the way it happens. **A chronological plot,** also called **organic or linear plot,** is a story structure that unfolds from start to finish the way it happens.

Let's take a scenario for example. A thief sneaks into a house and was caught. He was beaten outside, naked. Then he was taken to the police station and jailed. This story has a chronological plot because it is written the way it happens.

Another example is a story about a woman who catches her husband having sex with her maid. She kills her maid and warns her husband, dearly if he dares tell the authorities. The story also is organic because it is written the way it happens.

EPISODIC PLOTTING

Episodic Plotting, also called **inorganic plotting,** is the act of structuring a story *not* the way it happens. **An Episodic plot,** also referred to as **inorganic plot,** is a storyline that doesn't unfold the way it happens.

This is usually the kind of plot found in mystery, detective and crime stories. In fact, everyone tends to use this plot. I don't see any story I write that doesn't lean on the episodic plotting.

Let's examine a case where the previous organically plotted stories becomes inorganically plotted.

The story of the thief may begin from where he was being beaten outside, naked. Then continue on how he sneaked in and was caught. And end with how he was jailed.

The story of the murderous woman may begin with when she killed her maid and warned her husband. Then continue with how she caught her husband having sex. Maybe it would end up in her husband finally telling the cops.

The storylines above are non-linear

because...

What Makes a Story Plot Episodic

You may be wondering how storylines can be converted from organic to inorganic. The answer is a **flashback. A flashback,** like we see in movies, is a storytelling technique that introduces events that had happened before the time the current scene took place and the story would still flow.

Let's reconsider the two stories above.

The story of the thief began from where he was being beaten on the street, naked. Either the narrator or the thief himself or the person who caught him **flashbacked** (remembered how he sneaked in and was caught.) Then the narrator continues with how he was taken to the police station and jailed.

The story of the murderous woman began with how she killed her maid and warned her husband. Then either she or the narrator would **flashback** (remember how she caught her husband having sex with the maid.) Then the narrator continues with the husband actually disobeying her and telling the cops.

How to Spot a Flashback in a Story

It is so easy to say flashback was why the story became episodic. But when it comes to spotting them, some have difficulties doing that.

Let's use an excerpt from one of my stories, *Unknown Identity:*

"
Latifat staggered along in

the dark night, gazing up at the bluish-black sky littered with glinting stars. She managed to keep her pace consistently on the narrow street with cars parked here and there. She muttered some things inaudibly, to the disgust of occasional passersby. Under her round-neck top, she hid her ever sweet gin.

A few more meters and she would be home.

She looked up again as she stopped her utterly disoriented manner of walking. Her family's rented apartment was over there, gigantic as it could be. It was fondly referred to as a barracks by the people llliving in the neighborhood.

Am I really dreaming*, she thought.*

No one to answer that, of course.

She stopped, looked back to find no one.

What nonsense! But I'm sure I said it out.

Common sense told her she should forget the past and just head home.

> *She continued staggering home as the thought of the evening flooded her. Even in her state of sub consciousness, she knew what happened.*
>
> *Earlier at 5 pm, she had rolled back and forth on the sofa in the living room. Her father had stormed out from the inner room and gave her some hot slaps*
>
> **"**
>
> *on her back.*

The highlighted phrase above marks the commencement of the flashback scene.

In Stephen King's *A Death,* a flashback scene begins when the author wrote:

> **"**
>
> *Prosecutor Mizell called half a dozen witnesses, and Judge Mizell never objected once to his line of questioning. Mr. Cline testified first, and Sheriff Barclay came last. The story that emerged was a simple one. At noon*

> *on the day of Rebecca Cline's murder, there had been a birthday party, with cake and ice cream.* Several of Rebecca's friends had attended. Around two o'clock, while the little girls were playing Pin the Tail on the Donkey and Musical Chairs, Jim Trusdale entered the Chuck-a-Luck and ordered a knock of whiskey. He was wearing his plainsman hat. He made the drink last, and when
>
> **"**
>
> it was gone he ordered another.

The sentence above also welcomes a flashback scene, which was at noonday of Rebecca Cline's murder. Actually, he committed the crime before he was arrested and tried.

Self-assessment 1

Outline the storyline of your story based on the character, conflict and setting ideas you had in chapter one. If you are not an outline buff, then you can just note where you will have a flashback scene or not. It's even no use to outline if you're writing a linear plot. And on a second note, remember that there's no right way or wrong way to deal with your story.

If you'd want to write an inorganic storyline, use a hierarchy to outline it. Like the one below.

- The thief was being beaten.
  - he sneaks in.
  - he was caught.
- He was taken to the police station.
- He was jailed.

SUMMARY

In this chapter, you have learned:

- What plots are.
- The types of plots.
- What makes a plot episodic.
- How to spot a flashback scene in a story.

Self-assessment 2

By this time, you should have a completed storyline for the character, conflict and story ideas you had in chapter one. if you don't, kindly go back and complete the self-assessment tests.

The Ultimate Guide on How to Write a Short Story

CHAPTER *3*

DIALOGUE

INTRODUCTION

In a work of prose fiction, a writer doesn't only write what happens, he or she writes what the characters said, too. Dialogue is a great way to move a plot forward, especially if it is used to reveal something.

Dialogues are great because...

- ...they let you into the scene pictorially. While reading a work with dialogue, it's one of the elements that makes you feel as if you're present at the scene.

- ...they make the characters realer. Once a reader keeps with the flow of dialogues in a story, even without exclamation marks, the reader will know when a certain character is angry or shouting.

- ...they make readers remember characters in a story. It's the unique way a character speaks that works the magic. If anything the character said resonates with a reader, the reader quickly remembers him or her.

- ...they move the plot forward. As a writer, you shouldn't always get in the way of the characters in your story. You should let them speak. Or rather make them speak for you. You may not want to reveal a truth, but with a dialogue. And the truth can determine where your story recourse to.

DIALOGUE PUNCTUATION

While reading other authors, nothing disgusts me more than an ocean of jam-packed punctuation errors. In order to understand the way a dialogue works, we'll be looking into the lesson of its punctuation.

Lesson one: Every dialogue deserves a quote

Unless you are a writing expert and you wants to break the rule for a purpose, I'll advise you to abide by it. Great writers like Chinua Achebe, Stephen King, etc., abide by the rule.

Ideally, a dialogue should look like:

"I'm going home," Cassidy said.

"Well, I know you would say that. It's always in your blood."

"No, mother. I am honest."

Lesson two: Tell us who's talking with dialogue tags

In a story where the plot depends much

more on dialogue, there would be lots of them in it and it would be a big mistake to let reader start thinking, "That's the cops who just spoke. Ariel hasn't said anything, so this would be her mother talking."

Ah, enough. Unless it is obvious who's talking, use dialogue tags to indicate the speaker. Dialogue tags are phrases outside the dialogue quote that modifies the quoted words, like identifying the speaker, specifying an action associated with what the speaker said.

The tags range from...

- ...said.
- ...asked.
- ...replied.
- ...told.

After the tags, a comma may be added and then additional information may be given to help understand the words inside quote better.

For example:

"We're not going anywhere," Alan said, stepping forward.

"Huh?" the sheriff said, surprised.

"Oh," Alan's mother said and stifled a laugh. "Don't mind him, sheriff. He's just boyish."

"Well, Mrs. Peterson, we have no time to waste," the sheriff replied.

Lesson three: Give every speaker their own paragraph

This lesson is just as simple as the wordings. Did you notice how words of different speakers in the above dialogues are on different paragraphs? It does one thing, helps your reader to identify a specific speaker's words.

Lesson four: Introduce a dialogue tag with a comma inside the quote, a space after the quote and a full stop exactly where the tag ends.

For example:

"I am going home," Hattie

said.

What I was actually referring to is the comma after the "home", the space after the quotation mark and the full stop after "said".

Lesson five: Separate different sentences in a dialogue with a comma inside the first quote and a full stop outside it

I'm quite sure you'll want to have a line of dialogue like this one I had below:

> *"Oh," Alan's mother said and stifled a laugh. "Don't mind him, sheriff. He's just boyish."*

Did you notice the comma after the "Oh"? and the full stop behind "laugh"? That makes that a complete sentence, because of the full stop. If you were to only write the words of Alan's mother, it would be:

> *Oh. Don't mind him, sheriff. He's just boyish.*

If it were: *Oh, don't mind him, sheriff. He's just boyish,* the line of dialogue will look like:

> *"Oh," Alan's mother said and*

stifled a laugh, "don't mind him, sheriff. He's just boyish."

Lesson six: Use only commas when, in a line of dialogue, a sentence hasn't been completed. Only use a full stop when it's complete.

For example, consider the following words: Why would he, Obinna, of all people, be plagued without even knowing the evil doer, which, in his village, is a great abomination.

The line of dialogue infused with a tag would look like this:

"Why would he, Obinna," he said, "of all people, be plagued without even knowing the evildoer, which, in his village, is a great abomination."

That leaves the impression that a comma only divides a character's speech and a tag; a character's speech, a tag, which is followed by the character's remaining speech, to complete the sentence before a full stop is now used.

Lesson seven: Always capitalize the first word of a noun in a tag

"*I am going home,*" *Hattie said.*

Lesson eight: Always treat an exclamation and a question mark like a comma

For example, a line of dialogue with question marks and exclamation should look like this:

"*Are you home?*" *he asked.*
"*Am I home?*" *Hattie asked.*
"*What!*" *he exclaimed.*

Lesson nine: Never capitalize any other word other than noun

For example, it shouldn't be:

"*Okay,*" *The sheriff said.*
"*Let's go to town.*"

It should be:

"*Okay,*" *the sheriff said.*
"*Let's go to town.*"

Lesson ten: If you want to use a dialogue tag, either use a comma, exclamation or question tag inside the quote, not a full stop

- ✓ "I am going home," Hattie said.
- ✓ "Are you talking to me?" the ogre asked.
- ✓ "What!" Bush exclaimed.

- ✗ "I am going home." Hattie said.
- ✗ "We're not going anywhere." the boy exclaimed.

Note: For better understanding and analysis of dialogue punctuations, pull out novels on your shelf and start seeing for yourself. Otherwise, this fail-proof pattern below is yours to the rescue.

Fail proof pattern formula

- Write down the bare words your character says without any quote or tag. Like these below.
  - I am going home.

- We're going nowhere.
- Oh. Don't mind him, sheriff.
  He's just boyish.
- Determine the point you want to put
  your tag if any. Like these below.
  - I am going home[tag here].
  - We're going nowhere[tag here].
  - Oh[tag here]. Don't mind him, she-
    riff. He's just boyish.
- Insert your tags preceded by a comma
  and a space respectively. Like these be-
  low.
  - I am going home, Hattie said.
  - We're going nowhere, he said.
  - Oh, Alan's mother said and
    stifled a laugh. Don't mind
    him, sheriff. He's just boyish.
- Wear the words that are not hig-
  hlighted with quotes. Like below.
  - "I am going home," Hattie said.
  - "We're going nowhere," he said.
  - "Oh," Alan's mother said and
    stifled a laugh. "Don't mind him,
    sheriff. He's just boyish."

Self-assessment 1

Have you written a story before? If yes, go back to it and reformat the dialogue punctuations well using the lessons or the fail-proof formula. Are you just going to start your story? Well, keep the lessons and formula handy.

CHARACTER'S VOICE

As plenty as human beings are, each still has a unique DNA code. Like that code, every writer, no matter how plenty we may be, has a unique voice. That's what is referred to as a **writing voice.**

The way I write is different from the way you will write. And the way you write is definitely different from the way a famous author will write. That concept of writing, sadly, isn't replicated in characters enough.

Sure, you want your character to look real. Sure, you'll try all your possible best to give your characters a fair share of dialogue, but it's not enough if they aren't unique. For the skeptics asking if giving every character in a story a unique voice is possible, let me give an interesting example.

There was this lady in my church that I do remember for the word, "like." Whenever there was a discussion and she wants to contribute, she could never let go of that word. A statement could go like this:

> *"Although, I went there myself and saw everything with my naked eyes, I was like, 'Is this really what they are going to do?'"*

She also uses the same words if she wants to report another person's speech.

> *"The girl saw me and was like, 'Hey, girl. Where have you been since all these days?'"*

Now, let's get this straight. I investigated myself and this is what my own speech would have looked like:

> *"Although, I went there and saw everything myself, I was still doubting whether that was what they were going to do."*

"The girl saw me and asked, 'Hey, girl. Where have you been?'"

Can you spot the difference? Yes, there's no problem if your character uses "like" or not. The problem is if all your characters sound the same. The solution? Take time to imagine what each of your characters are? Complete the character questionnaire, add your own questions, too (because I don't know everything on your mind or about your story.)

In chapter one, I gave about five ways to generate character ideas. One of them was to observe people wherever you are or go. Where are you now?

At home? Listen in to what your neighbors are saying and how. What about people on the street. At work? Can you just stroll to the cafeteria and listen to what people are saying there and how?

The idea works. Everytime.

While writing your dialogue also, you should also be mentally daydreaming about what you're writing. You should frame your inner mind and re-project your eyes to the scene. By that way, you'll just be a reporter, reporting what happens in your story.

It's good to write in solitude, away from earth's distractions. Maybe you enjoy music while writing. Or coffee. Or a quiet place. Make sure you're distractions free and plunge yourself into your story's scene and forget everything else.

Self-assessment 2

For the characters you have created in chapter one, create a brief summary of their voices (something you can glance over and remember maybe after you get back to your story or take a break.)

The Talking Head Syndrome

The talking head syndrome occurs when only lines of dialogue continue appearing in a story, without any hint of the character's action, the description of the setting or the changes occurring in the background.

The following dialogue is an example of where the talking head syndrome occurs.

> *"What is all this? Don't you realize you're wasting my time?"*
>
> *"I'm sorry my princess, but—"*
>
> *"But what?!"*
>
> *Yeye girl, the driver thought.*
>
> *"Ehen? But what?" she asked.*
>
> *"There is a man inside who said the people all disagree."*
>
> *"He said they don't agree, or they all said?"*
>
> *"He said it."*
>
> *"On behalf of them all?"*
>
> *"Yes."*
>
> *"Who does he think he is?"*

Compare the version above with the version below.

> *Outside, the jeep's window rolled down again and the manager*

showed up, simultaneously. For a moment, the driver was fed up with playing with the window for years.

"What is all this? Don't you realize you're wasting my time?"

"I'm sorry my princess, but—"

"But what?!" She banged her fist on the vehicle's window pane. The hand bumped up back without a scratch and the manager cringed. The driver observed it from his rear view mirror and winked once, looking out through the window.

Yeye girl, the driver thought.

The princess' eyes reddened and she gazed down at the manager for some seconds. "Ehen? But what?" she asked.

"There is a man inside who said the people all disagree." He was trembling.

The princess frowned in surprise. "He said they don't agree, or they all said?"

"He said it."

"On behalf of them all?"

The manager nodded.

She signaled the nearest guard and the guard opened the vehicle's door which extended to a few inches away from where the manager stood. He backed away.

"Who does he think he is?" she asked no one in particular as she climbed down from the jeep, her high heels delicately resting on the pebbles, and walking briskly toward the staircase that led to the entrance door.

Which do you think will be more enjoyable? Of course, the latter version. The talking head syndrome makes the reader feel like a statue is speaking in a story, instead of a specific character. This, combined with a character's voice problem, could ruin the success of your story completely.

As a solution, let me offer a quick tip that'll help you.

The Ultimate Guide on How to Write a Short Story

Imagine your scene as you write your story. Ahem, you see, the above excerpt is from one of my stories, *Beyond Her Boundary.* When I was writing it, I was alone and I didn't notice what was going on till I finished the piece. Yes, just in a day. When you let your sixth sense work for you while writing, you'll see what amateurs can't see.

For example, in the above excerpt, the manager and the princess were both human. At least, I made them real in the stories. They could walk, run, laugh, and all ranges of emotions. That is why the princess could frown. In the previous version, she didn't. That is why the manager could cringe. That is why the princess could bang her fist on the car's window pane.

All those actions show that they are human. Now imagine your typical day.

Suppose a writer wants to write a scene that took place when you were having a conversation with someone. Were you in a static position then? Well, readers will assume you are if you don't write that down in the story. The story won't feel real. Readers don't want that. Readers want a story that will make them feel they are in another world.

People don't just do one thing alone these days. People multitask. Think of a single mother with three kids. If a writer were to write about her having a conversation with a business partner on the phone, we want to see her silent remorse when the food got burnt in the kitchen. We want to see her shushing one of the kids, or covering the cellphone's mic to address one of the kids. We want to see her tidying up the house, eating candy and talking to her ex-husband on the phone at the same time.

Self-assessment 3

Write a brief scene about you having a serious discussion with your mom or dad and look out for the character's voice problem and the talking head syndrome.

If you have written a story before, go through the dialogues and see if it matches the way it would have happened in reality. If not, re-imagine what the characters involve in that scene would have done, feel, hear, show, apart from speaking. Then include it.

SUMMARY

In this chapter, you have learned:

- How to punctuate a dialogue.
- How to give each character a unique voice in your story.
- How to avoid the talking head syndrome.

CHAPTER *4*

POINT OF VIEW

INTRODUCTION

A Point of view means from whose perspective the story is told. When we write stories, it is from someone's side we see it. It could be one of the characters. It could be the narrator, the writer, you in particular. It could be from the perspective of someone who knows the story inside out.

You too are going to write your story from the perspective of someone. But before you begin to meditate on which point of view you are going to use, you should know the types of point of view that writers can use to write a story.

TYPES OF POINT OF VIEW

Basically, there are three types of point of view namely, the first person, the second person and the third person point of view.

First Person Point of View

This entails writing a story from the point of view of one of the characters or your own if you are one of the characters. In this situation, there is frequent use of personal pronouns **I, me, my, mine, we,** and the like.

For example, Chimamanda Adichie Ngozi wrote her popular novel, *Purple Hibiscus,* from the point of view of one of the characters, Kambili a young girl. Everything that happens in that story either happened in the character's presence or is just an opinion of the character.

Example of a first person point of view story is one of my stories, *Jungle Choice,* which is a flash fiction:

> As I plunged my butt on a log of wood in the cold night, I suddenly felt the desire to make a choice, a choice between life and death. Oh, no. it wasn't that I wished for death; it was just that it could happen to me. Now that I was in the forest, alone, weary of any impending danger, my heart reeled and I suddenly chose life. Does that even flow together? I chose life, yet death is sure to run after me.
>
> I felt a movement behind me. I stiffened my body and held my

breath, still sitting. That was when I remembered the words of my father before he died.

"Harry, I want to ask you a fearful question, can I?"

I had dashed toward him in my youthful energy, eager to hear what the challenge was this time. "Of course. Or do you want to pay before asking me?"

He laughed. "I would gladly pay you, but not this time. Maybe later, with something prestigious."

"Huh?" I felt suddenly tired. At second thought, I mustered some courage and said, "Okay, dad, what's the question."

"Hmmm…" He paused and sighed. He looked at me and I was sure he saw something promising in my eyes. He finally said, "Harry, what if you find yourself alone in a jungle?"

When the memory faded away, I sprang up to my feet in a jump *and shouted to the empty silence, "I'll fight! I'll fight my way through to life."*

In the distant, I heard someone encouraging me. Perhaps it was my shadow. People call it echo.

Harry wrote the above story; at least, we can assume so. He narrated how his father asked him a question and gave a detailed opinion about what he thought about him. Some things I want you to note from the above story is:

- ...the format of the dialogue.
- ...the avoidance of the talking head syndrome.

Self-assessment 1

Choose one of your previously written stories, or pick up a scene from one of your favorite author's stories, or from the ideas you've got in chapter one, write a brief narration in a first person point of view. That means you act in place of the character, as I took Harry's place in the above story.

The Second Person Point of View

This is the most seldom used perspective in story writing. It entails a writer writing a story about a reader. In this kind of situation, the reader is reading about his or her story. There is a frequent use of pronouns like **you, yours, your,** and the like in this kind of story. The second person point of view version of my flash fiction story above is this:

> As you plunged your butt on a log of wood in the cold night, you suddenly felt the desire to make a choice, a choice between life and death. Oh, no. it wasn't that you wished for death; it was just that it could happen to you. Now that you're in the forest, alone, weary of any impending danger, your heart reeled and you suddenly chose life. Does that

even flow together? *You* chose life, yet death is sure to run after *you*.

You felt a movement behind *you*. *You* stiffened *your* body and held *your* breath, still sitting. That was when *you* remembered the words of *your* father before he died.

"Harry, I want to ask you a fearful question, can I?"

You had dashed toward him in *your* youthful energy, eager to hear what the challenge was this time. "Of course. Or do you want to pay before asking me?"

He laughed. "I would gladly pay you, but not this time. Maybe later, with something prestigious."

"Huh?" *You* felt suddenly tired. At second thought, *you* mustered some courage and said, "Okay, dad, what's the question."

"Hmmm…" He paused and sighed. He looked at *you* and *you* were sure he saw something promising in *your* eyes. He finally said, "Harry, what if *you* find yourself alone in a jungle?"

When the memory faded away, *you* sprang up to *your* feet in a jump and shouted to the empty silence, "I'll fight! I'll fight my way through to life."

In the distant, *you* heard someone encouraging *you*. Perhaps it was *your* shadow. People call it echo.

I think the pronouns speak for themselves. You can change any story from any point of view to the other. That was changed from first-person to second-person point of view.

Self-assessment 2

Change the point of view of the story you wrote in self-assessment 1 to second person.

The Third Person Point of View

It is also called the **omniscient point of view.** It is a perspective of a story from someone who knows the story inside out. The narrator doesn't get a chance to be named, so it was given an omniscient. Also, only God knows everything inside out, that's why the name fits better.

We often hear about the attribute of God, that he's omniscient (being everywhere and knowing everything.) Since that is the attribute the narrator commands in respect to the story, it has to be called omniscient.

In this kind of story, the narrator knows everything about a story, chooses what to reveal or not, and how. There is a frequent use of pronouns like **he, she, they, his, her, him, their,** and the like.

A third person point of view version of my flash fiction story above is this:

> As he plunged his butt on a log of wood in the cold night, he suddenly felt the desire to make a choice, a choice between life

and death. Oh, no. it wasn't that he wished for death; it was just that it could happen to him. Now that he was in the forest, alone, weary of any impending danger, his heart reeled and he suddenly chose life. Does that even flow together? He chose life, yet death is sure to run after him.

He felt a movement behind him. He stiffened his body and held his breath, still sitting. That was when he remembered the words of his father before he died.

"Harry, I want to ask you a fearful question, can I?"

He had dashed toward him in his youthful energy, eager to hear what the challenge was this time. "Of course. Or do you want to pay before asking me?"

He laughed. "I would gladly pay you, but not this time. Maybe later, with something prestigious."

"Huh?" He felt suddenly tired.

At second thought, he mustered some courage and said, "Okay, dad, what's the question."

"Hmmm..." He paused and sighed. His dad looked at him and he was sure his dad saw something promising in his eyes. He finally said, "Harry, what if you find yourself alone in a jungle?"

When the memory faded away, he sprang up to his feet in a jump and shouted to the empty silence, "I'll fight! I'll fight my way through to life."

In the distant, he heard someone encouraging him. Perhaps it was his shadow. People call it echo.

Types of the Third Person Omniscient Point of View

1. **The third person omniscient point of view:** In this type of third person perspective, the narrator only narrates what happens in the story. The narrator cannot add his or her

comment or opinion to the story.

2. The third person objective point of view: In this type of third person point of view story, the narrator equally narrates and is free to comment and opine about happenings in the story.

Self-assessment 3

As you did in self-assessment 2, change the perspective of the brief narration to a third person omniscient point of view. You can make it objective by adding your own comments.

The Combination of two or more perspectives

It does happen that writers want to play around. And combining point of views in a story is a surefire way to learn and try new things. There's no compulsory way to combine perspectives. Some scene are just written in a point of view; while some are written in the other. The following are possible combinations of how you can combine point of views in your story.

- A first person and a third person omniscient.
- A first person and a third person objective.
- A first person and another first person.
- A first person and a second person.
- A second person and a third person objective.
- A second person and a third person omniscient.
- A second person and another second person.

As said earlier on, there is no right or wrong way to go about creative writing. You just have to try your hands on things till you find what is best for you. I know some writers who use four first-person points of view in their stories, so it's never bad if you invent your own.

The following is a combination of a third-person and a first-person point of view from one of my stories, *Unknown Identity*.

The Ultimate Guide on How to Write a Short Story

Her dad wore his pair of shoes, carried his bag on his left shoulder as it dangled along incoherently. "Make sure you're fully awake. I'm off to work."

That statement almost wanted to make me go crazy. All my life, I hadn't known anyone to call my mom. And my dad had never talked about anything related to her. The natural scar still lingered on in my heart, throbbing at my most excited moments. With me and my sister and dad, we kept pushing on.

My dad worked spontaneously. His working hours weren't exactly defined. Sometimes, he would work throughout the weekend. Sometimes, not. And many times, he had only had to go to work once in a week.

He was off to work now, on a night shift, and that means freedom for the night, and till dawn. I had slept at 12 pm

purposefully. I knew I'd need a sharp mind at my friend's birthday party tonight. It doesn't matter when it started, or when I got there. What matters was to be awake until I'm satisfied enough to leave to prepare for school.

School these days wasn't that exciting. My only prayer was to write my SSCE quickly and leave to battle life.

In a snap, Lattie was on the house chores. Before Zainab would return from the neighbor she'd gone to watch TV, she planned to prepare her food.

Can you see the indication of a shift in perspectives with the bold letters? I know a writer who just begin a scene with the character's name and tell the tale in the character's point of view. Something like:

CHARACTER ONE

Character one's point of view story here.

CHARACTER TWO

Character two's point of view story here.

CHARACTER THREE

Character three's point of view story here.

CHARACTER FOUR

Character four's point of view story here.

SUMMARY

In this chapter, you have learned:

- ...what a point of view is.
- ...the types of point of view.
- ...how to write in each point of view.
- ...how to combine point of views.

Self-assessment 4

Now is the time to choose the point of view that you want to write your story in. Choose a point of view each for the ideas you have gotten in chapter one, or in addition to the outline in chapter two. Don't forget that as you write, you'll need dialogues, so don't forget to keep the lessons and the fail-proof formula in handy.

DID YOU LIKE THIS BOOK?

Let everyone know by posting a review on Amazon. Just open the below link in your browser and it will take you directly to the reviews page where you'll write your review. It'll take less than five minutes:

http://amzn.to/22hz69r

OTHER BOOKS BY THE AUTHOR

I have written a few books in the Young Writers' Craft Guides series. You can see them by opening this link in your browser: http://bit.ly/1Ou19fw

Generate and Validate Your Bestselling Book Idea.

From the Author

Let me just put it simply that if I'd had a kind of book like this when I was starting out, I would have been smelling bestsellers, if not had many bestsellers.

And I want to help you avoid that.

Writing a book starts with an idea: you have to

have lots of it and then validate it (confirm that it would sell) before proceeding. But many authors are out there, confused as to where to find ideas they can turn into books that'll sell.

Some are plain scared (and/or lazy) to go the extra mile because either all the ideas they have aren't going to sell or that they feel they can't write a book on the ideas they keep getting.

Some are plain stuck. "So I've got this idea," they say, "where to?" Well, that's what this series will answer.

You should be able to look at the books in this series and know the next step you need to take. You should be able to read those books and know exactly what to do.

For a moment, forget about the distractions out there. You need quantity as much as you need quality, and it's all distilled here for you.

As you apply what's in this book, may you find joy in everything you write.

Excerpt from the Book

4 TIPS FOR FINDING BOOK IDEAS

The Ultimate Guide on How to Write a Short Story

If you want your book to stand a chance in the hell of iceberg of books out there, you have to focus on some core things. I believe if you can generate a unique book idea, find a tantalizing and attention-grabbing title, and write emotion-driven sales copy, you have given yourself a whole lot of chance against your competitions.

It's not the only thing, I know. But how many authors would do it?

"Do what?" you ask.

Do spend time to find ideas. Some authors are quite lazy that they couldn't even jot down ideas that pop into their brain. They think they can't forget it. They think it's crap. They it's too simplistic. Or, a whole lot of other vague reason.

It once happened to me. Why? Because I had so many ideas I didn't work on. It came to a time that I had to get rid of a whole jotter full of ideas, both fiction and nonfiction. And you know what? I think it's a terrible mistake. I still regret it.

How many authors would spend time to jot ideas? It doesn't matter whether they're in the bathroom, eating, or taking a walk in the Sahara Desert. What matters is to capture the ideas.

Ideas are like birds. If you don't capture them when they gently, willingly perch on the small branch of a short tree in your garden, they'll fearfully, quickly fly away. And maybe you caught a glance of them while moving away. But that's not enough. Nothing equates the presence of that bird.

To worsen the matters more, how many authors would validate their ideas? I mean, how many would look at the eBook market and see with their naked eyes that their ideas are needed?

You see, writing a book based on an idea that the market doesn't approve of is like going around, checking in front doors of people and proposing a literature to them when they have five kids at home giving them a hell of problem. Right then... I mean, right then, all they need is someone who'd help calm their kids. So to hell with... was it literature or something?

Alas! It could be an author's book. Specifically, it may be your book. How sad is that?

How many authors would research other books already published, and offer a different solid perspective? Or cater to another demographic entirely?

You see, Amazon Kindle has made life better. You could look inside as many books as have the "Look Inside" feature and see the quality of the book right away. It's not like the good ol' days when you had to buy the physical books yourself. Sure, you may check it out at bookstores. But how many bookstores would you want to visit everyday to gather the necessary research for your book.

You can't spend the whole eternity there.

Furthermore, how many of that book do you think that bookstore would have? Oh, don't you see other books competing for attention? Recipe books, weight loss books, make money, save money, invest money, and build financial wealth books, and a host of fiction books. Oh my.

Then it's the matter of other eBook platforms. Could you please "Look Inside" a Kobo eBook before you buy?

That is why you shouldn't rush to write that book. Yoou should sit, think, list out a range of ideas, and check the internet for validation.

I have something for you. So here we go.

1. Observe People's Problem

Okay, it sounds so ridiculous. I can feel it even as I'm writing this. But it works.

Think of these scenarios.

The Ultimate Guide on How to Write a Short Story

An introvert who curls up on his bed 24/7 without an ounce of courage to explore the outdoors, for... whatever reasons.

A beginning writer who's furiously searching the internet for how to publish an eBook with minimal expenses.

A fat housewife who's hellbent on losing weight to please her husnand.

Something is common to these people: they have a problem. The question is, can you solve that problem? If you ask me, it starts with you observing their problem, even if they don't come to you.

That introvert needs some inspirational book to lift his spirit. Or perhaps a funny story to lighten his mood.

That beginner needs information on

publishing eBooks, distilled in an easy-to-read, easy-to-navigate eBook like the one he/she wants to publish.

That housewife needs techniques that work to combat her excess fat.

They all want the same thing: solution to their problems. And the first step you can take is to observe it. In other words, understand them, understand the problem, understand the emotions that rolls with it, understand anything worth understanding about them and their problem.

2. Try Solving the Problems

This is the sequel to #1. Why not try to solve those problems? You've seen the problems, experienced it, understood it.

Maybe you have an introvert brother. And let's assume, for a whole lot of sufficient and good reasons, that he's doing fine. How did he? Did you help with that? That's the answer to that introvert's problem. Personal stories with sprinkles of facts in it.

Maybe you've been a beginner, too. Once. Wait, you were a beginner at a point in time. Do you remember? That time when writing regularly was the hardest problem in the whole world. That time when you just wonder where your creative muse went to. That time when you stare at the screen, arms folded on your chest, waiting for inspiration.

Oh, what about the horror of formatting your books? Publishing them? Promotion them? Arghh! You already have a series of book ideas.

Maybe you were once fat. Or maybe you know how to lose weight fast. There. That's it.

Can I tell you the truth? It's never simpler than that. And wait, it's never more complicated than that. End of story.

3. Pick Your Area of "Inpertise"

Lest I forget, I checked my dictionary, but I couldn't find the word "Inpert."

The word originated when I was brainstorming with my mentor. The idea was that since you're not an "expert" yet, you can be an "inpert." Which means that instead of wearing the same wig with a college professor, you can come off as reporting what ordeal you went through, how you learned what you're narrating now, what worked for you, and what did not.

Simply put, an **inpert** is:

Someone who doesn't appear as a Know-It-All, but who, with a conscious state of mind, commits to learning every day and helping others learn what he's also learned.

Your area of expertise can be anything. Remember that you're learning and the tribe following you is learning as you.

The Ultimate Guide on How to Write a Short Story

Have you been studying how to write a Kindle book lately, but you don't yet have a slew of Kindle books under your belt? You can relate your experience.

Tell us why your techniques didn't work, if it didn't. Tell us why it worked, if it did. Tell us the "smartcuts" you'd have taken to learn it faster. This itself opens door to whatever you've been learning, whether a hobby or not, and that you're passionate about.

4. Jot Every Idea

Do simply go out with your pen and notepad. If you're tech savvy (why wouldn't you be?), you have your smartphone with you all the time.

The truth about ideas vanishing won't appear real, until it happens to you.

Many times, I've had to rack my brain, even to

the point of physically hitting my head, telling my brain to dole out the idea I was looking for. Turns out, I was wrong. My brain wasn't the fault. In fact, I can atest that it was right then I began to recall everything I did in the twenty-four hour timeframe.

How I went to the bathrom, how I eat, all that. But not the words. Sometimes I'd remember it, sometimes not. But I'm urging you to save yourself brain-racking sessions by jotting every idea.

Have an idea of a military fiction? Jot it. What about weight loss? Jot it. How about making lots of money? Jot it. What about designing a book cover without designing skills? Jot it.

Two words: **jot it.**

It doesn't matter where you are or even how horrible the idea sounds. All of our idea sucks, but you'll discover how to know whether there's market for your book or not. Right now, jot that idea.

The Ultimate Guide on How to Write a Short Story
Click here to buy: http://amzn.to/1R2IQbR

ABOUT THE AUTHOR

Hello, I'm Abraham Adekunle, an eighteen-year-old writer, author, and upcoming online enterpreneurs.

I believe starting from scratch shouldn't be a hit-or-miss game for young writers and authorpreneurs like me, because it has been for me. But I started writing the Young Writers' Craft Guides Series to help with that.

Accordingly, writers should be able to look at that series and know the exact step they should be taking on their way to publishing. They should be able to read the books and do what it promised after they finish it.

That is my goal and it can't survive without your support. To join my email list, go to http://writewithabraham.blogspot.com

If you have any question you'd like to get my answer to, kindly forward it to youngwriterscraft@gmail.com